GOD
His Nature and Attributes

Bible Correspondence Course
FIRST OF A SERIES OF THREE

Charles H. Shofstahl

PLEASE CONTACT US AT:

**REVIVAL LITERATURE
PO BOX 505
SKYLAND, NC 28776
800-252-8896
www.revivallit.org**

ISBN 978-1-56632-016-0

Copyright © 1985, 2016 by Revival Literature. All rights reserved. No reproduction in any form of this book, in whole or in part, except for brief quotations in articles or reviews, may be made without written permission from Revival Literature, PO Box 6068, Asheville, NC 28816.

Printed in the United States of America.

GOD

In this day of confusion and doubt many people are searching for the answers to the problems of life. The basic idea being taught today is that man is the master of his own fate. This is humanistic philosophy and is the cause of all the confusion.

The purpose of this course of study is to seek the answers to the problems of life in the only place they can be found—THE BIBLE—and to turn people to look to God instead of man for the answers.

As you progress in your study of the Word of God, it is our prayer that you may come to a true knowledge of God as He reveals Himself in His written Word, the Bible. As you come to know and obey Him, you will find that your doubts and confusion have been replaced with faith and purpose, and a wonderful change has taken place in your life. Your whole life will be affected as you become established on solid, godly principles of Bible faith.

The first change that must take place in your life before you can grow spiritually is spiritual rebirth. You must be BORN AGAIN.

> "Except a man be born again, he cannot see the kingdom of God." (John 3:3)

In order for a person to exercise saving faith, he must know certain facts. He must know something about God, sin and man. Sin separates God and man. To understand sin, we must know something about God and His holy nature and demands. Therefore, our study commences with God.

Let us bow our hearts and seek the heart and mind of God as we seek to know Him. The "Sweet Psalmist of Israel," King David, more than 3,000 years ago, uttered this prayer:

> "Open thou mine eyes, that I may behold wondrous things out of thy law." (Psalm 119:18)

Man of himself is incapable of discovering God (1 Corinthians 2:14), and so God must reveal Himself to man.

> "Thy hands have made me and fashioned me: give me understanding, that I may learn thy commandments." (Psalm 119:73)

Other books reveal what men have learned. History, science, philosophy—all containing SOME TRUTH concerning God—are not enough to lead a person to know God. History tells how God has dealt with man down through the ages. Science reveals what little bit man has discovered about God's wonderful creation. And philosophy is man's guesses about the meaning of life—and there are as many guesses as there are men. But there is only one true and complete knowledge of God, Who is the Almighty and holy LORD of His creation, the universe (Psalm 139). To know God you must look into the Bible.

INSTRUCTIONS

The passages quoted and referred to in this study are taken from the Authorized Version (AV) of 1611, known as the "King James Version" of the Bible. Since all references are based upon this version, we suggest that you use it. Look up each Scripture reference and answer all questions. Try to answer in your own words where direct quotes are not asked for.

In this booklet we will consider God:

      I. **God is Glorious**
     II. **God is Sovereign**
    III. **God is Holy**
     IV. **God is Righteous**
      V. **God is Good**
     VI. **God is Supernatural**

I. God is Glorious

What is the chief end of man? Why am I here?

note "Man's chief end (purpose) is to glorify God, and to enjoy Him forever."
(Spurgeon's Catechism)

A. He is the God of Glory

1. **Acts 7:2** — [me] Who appeared to Abraham in Mesopotamia? The God of glory

2. **Isaiah 48:11** — How does God view His own glory in *note* relation to others? That he is the creator and we did nothing to serve it

B. Man is to Glorify God

1. **1 Chronicles 16:29** — "Give unto the LORD the glory *note* due his name: bring an offering, and come before him: worship the LORD in the beauty of holiness."

note 2. **1 Corinthians 10:31** — [me] Here we are told that whether we eat, drink, or whatever we do, we are to "do all to the glory of God."

note 3. **1 Corinthians 6:20** — Why are we to glorify God in our body and spirit? Because we were bought with a price

C. How is Man to Glorify God? What Does It Mean to Glorify God?   *explain*

— Appreciation
— Adoration
— Affection
— Submission

1. APPRECIATION—"To glorify God is to set God highest in our thoughts, and to have a venerable esteem of Him." (Thomas Watson)

   a. **Psalm 92:8** — "But thou, LORD, art ~~most high~~ ~~above the earth~~ for evermore."
   "To glorify God is to have God-admiring thoughts; to esteem Him most excellent, and search for diamonds in this rock only." (Thomas Watson)

   b. **Psalm 97:9** — God is described as most high above the earth and far above all gods.

2. ADORATION or WORSHIP — To worship means to recognize and honor by bowing oneself before. Worship is due only to God—not man or angels—because only God is the divine and perfect One.

   a. **Acts 10:25-26** — Because Peter refused worship, we conclude that we are not to worship man.

   b. **Revelation 19:10; 22:8-9** — Even angels refuse worship; we worship only God.

   c. **Nehemiah 8:6** — How did Ezra and the people worship? Saying amen and lifting their hands and bowed their heads to the ground

   d. **John 4:23-24** — What is God called? Father and Spirit

   How do true worshippers worship God? in spirit and in truth

3. AFFECTION—LOVE

   a. **Matthew 22:35-38** — How are we told to love God? "Thou shalt love the Lord thy God with all thy _heart_, and with all thy _soul_ _and strength_."

   b. **Matthew 22:38** — How does God classify this? _it is the first and go cup comanmant_

   c. **John 14:15** — How do we demonstrate our love to God? (underline correct answer)

      (1) by telling Him we love Him

      (2) by obeying Him

      (3) by going on pilgrimages

      (4) by going to church

4. SUBMISSION—To be in submission means to bow before Him as your Lord. If He is your Lord, you are to be subject to Him.

   a. The Ten Commandments—the Moral Law of God—are found in Exodus 20:2-17. Who does God call Himself in verse 2? _the lord your God_

   b. **Romans 10:3** — How did Israel fail to submit themselves to God's righteousness? (underline correct answer)

      (1) They set up their own standard of right and wrong

      (2) They refused to call Him "LORD"

      (3) They blasphemed God's Name

      (4) They worshipped idols

God is glorious and demands that His creatures give Him the glory due unto His Name. It is only right that we bow in humble adoration and worship Him in all His glory.

II. God is Sovereign

note To say that God is *sovereign* is to say that God is GOD. He has created this universe, and He does in it as He pleases.

- **Revelation 4:11** — Why were all things created? _because of his will and for his power_

- **Genesis 1:3** — In creating light, and in all His creation, how did God accomplish it? (Underline the correct answer}

    note
    — He began a gradual evolutionary process
    — (He spoke things into existence)
    — The world was here when God arrived on the scene

note - **Proverbs 16:4** — Why did God make all things? _for himself_

- **Psalm 103:19** — "The LORD hath prepared his throne in the heavens; and _his kingdom rules over all_."

A. He is Sovereign over the Natural Elements

1. Among other things, Psalm 89:5-12 teaches that God can control the sea. ((TRUE)/FALSE)

2. **Psalm 104:20-31** — God is LORD of all His creation, including the animal kingdom.

    Where do the lions seek their food? _from God_

    God has the life and death of all animals in His hand. ((TRUE)/FALSE)

3. **Matthew 10:29** — God directs the life and death of even __*2 sparrows*__.

B. God is Sovereign over Spiritual Beings—Both Good and Bad

1. **1 Chronicles 21:15** — God sent an angel to _destroy_ Jerusalem, but turned from doing such a thing, and commanded the angel to stop.

2. How did God deliver Peter from prison and certain death in Acts 12:5-11? _He sent an angel_

3. In Matthew 8:28-34, the Lord Jesus Christ met a man who was the dwelling place of a great many demons. When they recognized Who He was, where did they request that He might send them if He cast them out?
   herd of swine
   Notice that they were bound to obey Him.

C. He is Sovereign over Human Governments

1. **Proverbs 21:1** — "The king's heart is in the _hands of the Lord like the rivers of water_" He leads and controls as He chooses.

2. **Psalm 75:6-7** — Human governors are placed into such positions by God Himself, who "_puts down_ one and _exalts another_."

3. **Daniel 4:17, 25, 32** — God places only men who know and love Him into positions of leadership in this world. (TRUE/**FALSE**)

D. God is Sovereign over the Individual Affairs of Men

1. **Genesis 45:3-8** — Joseph's brothers had sold him into slavery in Egypt. Yet, many years later, when they came face to face, whom did Joseph say had sent him to Egypt? _You_

    For what purpose? _because they were jealous at his popularity_

2. **Genesis 50:20** — Joseph told his brothers that even though they had intended _evil_, God meant it for _good_. Therefore, we see that God overrules men's evil schemes for His own glory and brings good out of them.

3. Who was the *anointed one* in Acts 4:24-30? _Jesus Christ_ (The Greek word for *anointed* is *Christos*.) Herod, Pontius Pilate, the Gentiles, and the people of Israel all united to carry out God's predetermined will. (TRUE/FALSE)

4. **Proverbs 16:9** — Even though men may think that their schemes and thoughts are their own, the course of their lives is directed by _the Lord_.

5. **Psalm 66:7** — God is supreme ruler of His creation, in spite of man's feeble strivings. Those who would exalt themselves are called _Rebellious_.

God—not man—is the center of the Universe.
Do you recognize the sovereignty of God?

III. God is Holy

God is PERFECT. Everything about Him is good and right. He is absolutely pure and clean from moral defilement. He is free from evil or iniquity. This is HOLINESS.

note **A. God Claims to be Holy**
   Leviticus 11:44, 45 — God here calls upon His people to be holy because _he is holy_

   To *sanctify* means to set something apart for a holy purpose, or to cleanse something from pollution or iniquity.

B. God's Dwelling Place is Holy

note 1. **Psalm 20:6** — Where does God hear from? _from heaven_

note 2. **Psalm 43:3** — God sends out His light and truth to lead people to worship Him on earth. Mount Zion, the place of the Temple, and the dwelling-place of God among His people Israel, is called _holy hill_

3. In Matthew 4:5 the city of Jerusalem is called _holy city_

C. Angels Proclaim His Holiness

note In the heavenly vision of the prophet in Isaiah 6:3, what did the angels (seraphim) cry as they flew before the LORD? _holy, holy, holy, is the Lord of hosts. The earth is full of his glory_

Read Revelation 4, and notice especially verse 8. The *beasts* refer to angels. Also see Ezekiel 1.

D. Men are to Proclaim God's Holiness

1. In his song of deliverance after Israel's miraculous crossing of the Red Sea in Exodus 15:11, Moses sang, "Who is like unto thee, O LORD, among the gods? who is like thee, _you gloriousness_, fearful in praises, doing wonders?"

2. In Psalm 30:4, what are the saints of the LORD to sing and give thanks for? _h.s holy name_

3. What is the name of the LORD in Psalm 111:9?
   holy and awesome

E. God's Fellowship is with Holy People

1. Habakkuk 1:13 says that God's eyes are too pure to look upon _of wrong_.

2. **1 Peter 1:15-16** — How are Christians supposed to act? (Choose one)

   a. To be holy most of the time

   b. To confess their sins twice a year—before Christmas and Easter

   c. To always be as holy as God in all things

   d. It really doesn't matter; God will forgive you if you sin

3. **Psalm 24:3-4** — What is required of the man who desires fellowship with God? _____

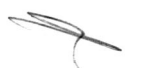

4. **Psalm 51:10** — To be restored to fellowship with God, a sinner must desire a right spirit and a _____ ~~.~~

F. **God's Love of Holiness is Demonstrated by His Actions toward and Demands of Israel**

note — *Moses at the burning bush*

1. **Exodus 3:5** — Why did God command Moses to take off his shoes? *because it's holy ground* _____ (see also Joshua 5:15)

2. **Exodus 26:33** — In this tabernacle in the wilderness, two rooms were divided by a vail.

    What were the two rooms called? *holy place* / *most holy*

note 3. **Exodus 28:36-38** — Aaron, the high priest, wore a mitre (priest's hat) as he ministered in the tabernacle. On the mitre was a solid gold plate engraved with *HOLINESS TO THE LORD*.

note 4. **Exodus 20:8-11** — The Ten Commandments reveal God's love for holiness and give us an idea of how man can be holy and please God. The fourth commandment states that God has sanctified a certain day. What did God do on the seventh day of His creation? *he rested* "wherefore the LORD blessed the sabbath day, and *hallowed* it."

note — *sacred, revered, holy, consecrated*

5. **Matthew 6:9** — How did Jesus instruct His disciples to consider the name of their Heavenly Father? *hallowed be your name*

All the civil and ceremonial laws of Israel in Exodus, Leviticus, and Deuteronomy show God's love for holiness. He required His people to be separated from all uncleanness.

G. God Hates Inquity (Sin)

1. **Leviticus 10:1-3** — When Aaron's two sons, Nadab and Abihu, failed to worship God in the way which God commanded, what did God do? _he consumed them_

2. **Leviticus 10:3** — What had the LORD told Moses? "I will be _sanctified_ in them that come nigh me, and before all the people I will be glorified." This was a great object lesson, showing God's love for holiness and hatred of sin (see verses 8-11).

3. **Romans 1:18** — What does God reveal from heaven against all unrighteousness and ungodliness of men? _his wrath_

4. **Romans 6:23** — Because God hates sin, what is the penalty for it? _death_

*Men must be separated from sin
or be separated from God*

H. God is Totally Holy

Psalm 145:17 — "The LORD is righteous in all his ways, and _kind in all his works_."

IV. God is Righteous

Righteousness is doing what is right. If God is perfectly holy, then His righteousness is measured by perfect holiness, and He will always do right.

A. All God's Dealings are Just and Right—He is a Righteous Judge

note 1. **Deuteronomy 32:4** — "A God of truth and without iniquity, _Righteous and upright_ is he."

note 2. **Psalm 97:2, 3** — As God dwells in holiness, so "_Righteous_ and _Justice_ are the habitation of his throne."

What does God do to His enemies round about Him? _burns them up_

B. God Demands that Sin be Punished

Because God is righteous and just in all His dealings, His holy nature prevents Him from simply forgiving sins indiscriminately.

note 1. **Psalm 11:6-7** — Why does the LORD punish wickedness and unrighteousness? _because he is righteous_

2. **Ezekiel 18:4** — Since all souls belong to God, each person is responsible to God; parents and children cannot assume the responsibility for each other's sins. "The soul that _sins_, it shall _die_."

Here we see the *justice* of God. He hates sin.

3. **Genesis 2:15-17** — What one tree did God command Adam not to eat the fruit of in the Garden of Eden? _the tree of the knowledge of good and evil_

   What was the penalty for disobedience? _death_

4. **Genesis 3:6** — Was Adam disobedient to God? _yes_
   Adam's disobedience resulted in a curse being pronounced upon God's creation which affected all mankind. This will be discussed more in Booklet No. 2, *Man and Sin*.

5. God pronounced a curse upon Adam and upon the ground for his sake. Even though he did not die physically the same day he disobeyed, he died spiritually. God drove them from His presence in the Garden—Genesis 3:17-24. At the same time, their bodies began to die physically because of the curse.

   God told them, "for _dust_ thou art, and unto _dust_ shalt thou return."

6. **Genesis 6:5-7** — What was the condition of man at this time? _evilness continually_

   What was the sentence God pronounced upon mankind because of this condition? _he will destroy man_

C. God's Judgments are Always Righteous

1. **Revelation 16:1, 5-7** — In the end times, the wrath of God will be poured out upon His enemies. Those who shed the blood of the saints will be forced to drink blood. The angel of the waters magnifies God for judging this way, and the one in the heavenly altar considers God's judgments _complete_.

2. **Psalm 9:16** — How is the LORD known? _____
   _____

>✧<
Righteousness is love of holiness.
Justice is hatred for sin.
>✧<

V. God is Good

Goodness represents God's dealings. He is holy, and therefore, He must be righteous. He is just and punishes sin. But He is also *good*. He aims to promote the happiness and welfare of His creatures.

- **Matthew 19:17** — Who alone is good? _God_

- [note] **Psalm 119:68** — "Thou art good, and _do good_"

- [note] **Psalm 52:1** — "The goodness of God _endures continually_"

- [note] **Psalm 107:1** — Why are we to give thanks unto the LORD? _for he is good_

- **Psalm 25:8** — What does the goodness of the LORD cause Him to do? _instruct sinners in the way_

- **Psalm 86:5** — What is God ready to do? _forgive_

What does He demonstrate plenty of toward all who call upon Him? _mercy_

- **Romans 2:4** — What is God's goodness designed to lead us to? _Repentance_

Repentance means a change of mind, which results in a turning away from sin and toward God and righteousness. This will be discussed in Booklet No. 3, *Salvation*.

- **Psalm 145:8-9** — "The LORD is _gracious_, and full of _mercy_; slow to anger, and of _abounding in tender mercy_. The LORD is good to _all_: and his _mercy_ are over all his works."

The goodness of God includes love, mercy, and grace.

A. LOVE—the expression of God's nature. God is the source of all love.

1. **1 John 4:16** — "God is _love_."
   The basis of God's love is His righteousness. Perfect love has a counterpart—perfect hatred. God loves righteousness and hates sin.

2. **Hebrews 1:9** — "Thou hast _loved righteousness_ and _hated sin_."

3. **John 3:16** — What did God's love for lost mankind cause Him to do with His Son? _Sent Him to die on the cross_

   Divine love is seen to be SACRIFICIAL. It is more than mere sentiment or warm feelings toward something that is "lovable." God chose to love that which is unlovely. _which is us_

4. **Romans 5:8** — What was our condition when God commended His love toward us? _sinners_

   God's goodness is demonstrated by His lovingkindness, which is the way He deals with those He loves.

5. Jeremiah 31:3 — "I have loved thee with an everlasting love: therefore with _I have continued my faithfulness to you_.

B. **MERCY**—compassion, pity, forbearance. God's mercy is demonstrated by the way He holds back from punishing sinners who deserve only punishment.

1. Psalm 145:8 — God's mercy is seen in that He is slow to _anger_.

2. Psalm 103:8-13 — God could justly punish all sin immediately, yet His mercy has caused Him to hold back His punishment. How has He dealt with us? _with mercy_

Mercy is longsuffering in action.

3. Lamentations 3:22 — How do God's mercy and compassions affect us? _they fail not_

C. **GRACE**—the bestowing of favor upon those who are undeserving. Anything God gives to man is on the basis of His grace. Man receives nothing because of his merits. Therefore, God is gracious.

1. What are man's righteousnesses compared to in Isaiah 64:6? _filthy rags_

2. Ephesians 2:8-9 — By what are we saved? _grace_

Why are man's works not included? _because it is nothing we have nor can earn_

God will not share His glory with others.

3. **Ephesians 2:6-7** — What was God's purpose in saving sinners? _So to our preach his word to glorify his name_

4. **Genesis 6:8** — Why was Noah saved from the flood? _he found grace in the eyes of the Lord_

5. **Exodus 34:6-7** — The LORD passed before Moses and proclaimed His glories. How many can you list?
   _6...._

*exceeding
usual limits*

VI. God is Supernatural

Super means *above*, therefore, *supernatural* means *above natural*. God is transcendent. He is beyond normal human experience. He cannot be detected by our natural physical senses (seeing, hearing, tasting, smelling, and feeling).

- **Isaiah 55:8-9** — Why can't man figure out God? *his thoughts and ways are greater than ours*

- **1 Corinthians 2:14** — How must God be perceived? _____

   A. **God is Spirit (John 4:24)**

   1. In Hebrews 12:9, He is also called the *Father of Spirits*.

   2. **1 Timothy 1:17** — God cannot be seen because He is *invisible*.

   B. **God is Unity**

   1. **Deuteronomy 6:4** — How many Gods are there? *one*

   2. **Isaiah 45:21-22** — Where must we look to be saved? *God, Jesus*
   How many Saviours are there? *1*

   C. **God is Trinity**

   1. **John 1:1** — Who dwelt in the beginning with God, and was God? *the word (Jesus Christ)*
   Stay in John 1:1

2. 1 Timothy 3:16 tells us that God was manifest in the flesh. (**TRUE**/FALSE)

3. **John 1:14** — What did the WORD become? *Jesus* *flesh*

4. What did Thomas call Jesus in John 20:28? *my Lord and my God*

5. In John 10:30, Jesus said that He was God (see verse 33). (**TRUE**/FALSE)

6. **John 5:23** — Can you worship the Father and yet refuse to worship the Son? *No*
The Council of Nice, in A.D. 325, condemned as heresy the doctrine known as ARIANISM, which taught that Jesus Christ was some creature higher than others, but lower than God.

7. **John 15:26** — Jesus talked of sending the *Comforter*, who is also called *the Spirit of truth*
Notice that the personal pronoun "he" is used, indicating reference to a person, rather than a force.

8. **Acts 5:3-4** — Peter said that Ananias lied to both *men and God*.
Such language indicates personalities.

The Trinity may be seen in several places.

9. **Matthew 3:16-17** — Who was baptized? *Jesus*

Who appeared like a dove? *The Spirit of God*
Whose voice was heard? *God*

24

10. **Matthew 28:19** — What name are believers to be baptized in? _Father, Son, Holy Spirit_

11. **1 John 5:7** — What three bear record in heaven? _Father, Son and Holy Spirit_ "and these _agree_ are _one_"

12. **Genesis 1:26** — "And God said, Let _US_ make man in _our_ image, after _our_ likeness"
    NOTE: The Hebrew Old Testament word translated here as "God" is *ELOHIM*, a word indicating *plurality*, so we see that more than one is present here.

>✧✦✧<
There are three persons in the Godhead
— But there is only one God
>✧✦✧<

D. God is Eternal
With God everything is "now". There is no time limit with God.

1. **Exodus 3:14** — God is called _I AM_

2. **Psalm 90:2** — How long has God been around? _from everlasting to everlasting_

3. **Revelation 1:8** — The one which is, was, and is yet to be is likened to the first and last letters of the Greek alphabet _alpha_ and _omega_.
   The New Testament was originally written in Koine, or common, Greek.

E. **God is Powerful**
God's power is unlimited. He never has any problems accomplishing His plans. He is eternal and unchanging and everywhere.

1. **Jeremiah 23:24** — What does God fill? _heaven and earth_

2. **Psalm 139:7-12** — Can a person hide from God? _no_

3. **Jeremiah 32:17** — Considering the world and all God's creation, we must say with Jeremiah, "_There is nothing_ too hard for thee."

4. **Psalm 94:9-11** — God knows all about His creatures. He knows the "_thoughts_" of man, that they are vanity."

5. **Proverbs 15:3** — "The eyes of the LORD are in _every place_, beholding the _evil_ and the _good_."

Self-Evaluation

1. Is my understanding of God greater now that I have completed this study? (YES)/NO

2. Has my use of the Bible improved through this study? YES/NO

3. What are some attributes of God? _Glorious sourish_
   Holy, righteous, good, surdnatural

4. In your own words, define the sovereignty of God.
   he has all power

5. In your own words, define the holiness of God.
   he is perfect, pure, and without sin

6. What is eternity? _no end or start_
   and it could be either life or death

7. At this point, how do you think a person can intimately and personally know God? (This answer can later be compared with what you have learned through this series of studies, so you can evaluate your progress.)

God is Great

We hope this introduction to God has given you a little bit of insight into His holy and almighty character. The world is perishing because people do not know God. He has given His revelation—but you must take the time and effort to search it out. We hope you will continue with the next study booklet and keep right on until you have completed them all.

God is above man's puny ideas of life. He is our Creator. He is powerful and eternal. He is ever present and knows everything that all men every where do or even think. Can we ignore such a great God?

God is holy, righteous and just. He cannot overlook sin, and He sets down guidelines for men to live by. He commands men to be holy, as He is holy and punishes them for disobedience. He is longsuffering; He does not always act immediately to punish sin, but gives men time to repent.

God has provided salvation by grace through faith in the person and work of His dear Son, the Lord Jesus Christ, who satisfied God's just demands for the punishment of sin by dying on the cross, the death of a sinner, though He was perfect and never sinned. In the following booklets it will be shown how man is sinful and depraved, at enmity with the holy God, and how God, in grace, has reconciled sinners to Himself through His Son.

Booklet No. 2 is entitled *Man and Sin*
Booklet No. 3 is entitled *Salvation*

Our prayer is that you might be saved.

Not unto us, O Lord of heaven,
    But unto Thee be glory given;
In love and truth Thou dost fulfil
    The counsel for Thy sovereign will;
Though nations fail Thy power to own,
    Yet Thou dost reign, and Thou alone.

The idol-gods of heathen lands,
    Are but the work of human hands;
They cannot see, they cannot speak,
    Their ears are deaf, their hands are weak;
Like them shall be all those who hold
    To gods of silver and of gold.

Let Israel trust in God alone,
    The Lord whose grace and power are known;
To Him your full allegiance yield,
    And He will be your help and shield;
All those who fear Him God will bless,
    His saints have proved His faithfulness.

All ye that fear Him and adore,
    The Lord increase you more and more;
Both great and small who Him confess,
    You and your children He will bless;
Yea, blest are ye of Him who made
    The heavens, and earth's foundations laid.

The heavens are God's since time began,
    But He has given the earth to man;
The dead praise not the living God,
    But we will sound His praise abroad,
Yea, we will ever bless His Name;
    Praise ye the Lord, His praise proclaim.

(Based on Psalm 115) — copied

This booklet is presented to you by:

Additional copies of this booklet are available from:
REVIVAL LITERATURE
P.O. Box 6068 • Asheville, NC 28816
USA
1-800-252-8896